Save Macdonald Hall

Gordon Korman

Illustrated by
Susan Gardos

SCHOLASTIC CANADA LTD.

Canadian Cataloguing in Publication Data

Korman. Gordon
  Save Macdonald Hall

ISBN 0-590-54237-0

I. Gardos, Susan.   II.Title.

PS8571.O78S38 1998   jC813'.54   C98-931452-9
PZ7.K67Sa 1998

Adapted for Literacy Place by Paul Kropp from *Beware the Fish*!

5 4 3 2 1   Printed and bound in Canada   9/9 0 1 2/0

Contents

Chapter 1

Much ado about spinach

"Yes! Okay! So we need another vegetable! But why spinach?" said Boots O'Neal in disgust.

"Stewed green leaves," agreed Bruno Walton. He pushed the spinach as far from the rest of his dinner as he could. "Last week they started serving raisins and figs instead of cake and ice cream. Now it's spinach instead of french fries. If this keeps up, I'll be the healthiest person ever to starve to death at this school. Yeccch!"

"You cannot possibly starve on this diet," put in Elmer Drimsdale. "It is perfectly balanced in terms of diet and taste." He carefully put some spinach into his mouth.

"You can die if you don't eat it," replied Bruno. "We're starving. This isn't *food*!"

"Seems to me that Macdonald Hall is doing a lot of cost-cutting lately," Boots said. "Yesterday, someone kicked a soccer ball onto the road and it got run over by a truck. End of ball — end of game. Can you imagine a school this size owning only one soccer ball?"

"They even cut our evening snack," complained Bruno.

"The science lab is low on materials and they aren't being replaced," Elmer added. "The big microscope has been broken for a week!"

Suddenly Bruno pounded the table with his fist. "Macdonald Hall was never like this before. Mr. Sturgeon always used to stand up for us and get us the things we needed. Why isn't he doing it now?"

Nobody answered.

Bruno turned to Larry Wilson. "Larry," he said, "when you're on duty around The Fish's office, keep on the lookout. If we can find out why this is happening, we can do something."

"You've got it," agreed Larry.

* * *

Just before midnight, a squeak broke the silence around Macdonald Hall. The window of Room 306 in Dormitory 3 opened, and Bruno Walton and Boots O'Neal jumped to the ground. They darted across the highway and climbed over the fence around Miss Scrimmage's Finishing School for Young Ladies.

Bruno picked up a bunch of pebbles and tossed them at a second-storey window. Cathy Burton's head appeared over the sill. "Your food will be right down," she called softly.

A few minutes later, a large paper bag came sailing out the window and landed at the boys' feet. On the bag was a message: *Happy eating! From Miss Scrimmage's Finishing School for Young Ladies. Cathy Burton and Diane Grant, Caterers.*

Boots looked up at the open window. "You've just saved a couple of lives," he called.

"Our pleasure," answered Cathy. She waved, then shut the window.

The boys grabbed the food and returned to Macdonald Hall. They climbed back up to their room, where Bruno hurled himself onto the bed. Suddenly, there was a terrified scream.

In the moonlight, Boots saw his roommate struggling with someone on the floor. Without thinking, he threw himself into the battle.

Arms and legs thrashed wildly. Grunts filled the room. Boots could feel his head being forced into a headlock. He reached out blindly, grabbed a foot and started twisting.

There was a click and the light came on. The arm around Boots's neck was Bruno's. The hand twisting Bruno's foot was Boots's. Larry Wilson was standing by the light switch, pale and shaking.

"Cut that light!" Bruno gasped. "Do you want The Fish on our necks?"

Larry switched off the light. "Sorry," he said.

"What are you doing in our room?" demanded Boots.

"You asked me to keep my ears open," Larry replied. "I came here to make a report. You guys were out, and I guess I fell asleep."

"What did you hear?" Boots asked.

"You aren't going to like this very much," Larry replied. "The Fish has given orders to close Dormitory 3."

There was a long moment of silence.

Bruno was the first to find his voice. "No," he said quietly. "He can't do that. This is our home."

"Yes, he can," replied Larry. "Tomorrow everybody will be getting new rooms."

"Why?" cried Bruno. "Why would The Fish do this to us? Why?"

"Well," said Larry, "no one has actually said so, but it looks to me as if they can't afford to run three dorms any more."

"Then let them close Dorm 1! Or Dorm 2!" wailed Bruno. "But not ours! It's not fair!"

"What if you get sent to one room and me to another?" worried Boots.

"No, no," Larry told them. "You two guys are both being sent to Room 201."

There was another shocked silence.

"Elmer Drimsdale!" Bruno and Boots howled at the same time. "We can't live with Elmer Drimsdale. He's crazy!"

"But you guys are friends of Elmer's."

"Yes, but that's a lot different from *living* with him!" Bruno exclaimed. "Elmer keeps ants! And fish in the bathtub! And plants all over the place! And he's always doing some experiment that takes up half the room! And he gets up at six in the morning!"

"What have we done to deserve this?" asked Boots in despair.

Nobody said anything for a minute. Then Bruno spoke thoughtfully. "You know," he said, "we're losing sight of the most important thing. If Macdonald Hall is going broke, we won't just be out of a dormitory. We'll be out of a school!"

"Could be," said Larry. "Today I took a phone call from a real estate company. Maybe the Hall is being put up for sale."

In the darkness of Room 306, Bruno's face took on a grim look. "That does it!" he said. "They're starving us, they're forcing us out of our dorm, and now they're selling our school right out from under us! We won't let this happen!"

Chapter 2

I never get caught

Bruno and Boots were finding it hard to leave Room 306. When they had finished packing up their stuff and loading it onto a bed, Bruno flopped down on his suitcase. "You go on without me," he said to Boots. "I'll be along later."

"Aw, come on," said Boots. "Let's just get it over with!"

Bruno pushed himself to his feet, and the two boys began to carry the bed towards Dormitory 2. They struggled into the building and down the hall to Room 201.

Bruno kicked the door open. "Hi, Elmer," he said glumly. "It's us. We're moving in."

Elmer was sitting at his desk, peering through a microscope and making notes.

"Hello," he said. "Come on in. You can put the bed right over — uh — where *can* you put the bed?"

The room was already filled from wall to wall. A large fish tank gurgled on top of the dresser. A huge, sand-filled aquarium — the home of Elmer's ant colony — sat beside it. Books were piled everywhere, and all sorts of strange-looking devices lined the walls. Plant pots stood on every surface. There was a fern, a trailing ivy, a Venus fly-trap, a desert yucca and a large cactus that was in flower. The only thing on the walls was a large diagram of the Pacific salmon. It was rumoured at Macdonald Hall that Elmer kept an endless supply of these in case the one in use became shabby.

Bruno looked around. "Why don't we move your electro-formionic impulse net-browser — or whatever it is?" he said.

"Oh, we can't do that," said Elmer. "It's bolted to the floor. You'll just have to put the bed in front of the door."

"But how will we get in and out?"

"Just climb over it," said Elmer. He peered at Boots through large, horn-rimmed glasses. "You don't mind, do you?"

* * *

"Macdonald Hall is in trouble," Bruno stated at the start of the meeting that night in Elmer's room. "The only hope of saving it rests with us, the Macdonald Hall Preservation Society."

The boys looked at him uneasily. Larry Wilson and Pete Anderson sat across from Bruno. Elmer Drimsdale and Boots made up the rest of the committee.

"Macdonald Hall is going down the tubes!" Bruno said. "They may even put it up for sale!"

"That's crazy," said Pete. "The Fish would never allow it."

"The Fish is only the headmaster," Bruno reminded him. "He doesn't own the place; he just works here. He's a victim too, just like the rest of us."

"I don't believe it," said Boots.

"Believe it," replied Larry. "I'm The Fish's office help. I'm around to hear what goes on in his office, and it's true."

"But what can we do?" asked Pete. "We're just students."

"Well, it seems to me," said Bruno, "that if we could do something really great, we'd get a

14

lot of coverage in the newspapers and on TV. Then we'd get all sorts of new students. Everybody will want to send their kids to a school where great things happen."

"What great things?" asked Boots.

"Well, that's going to be the hard part," Bruno admitted. "I haven't thought of any yet. We'll put up a suggestion box and talk it up a lot so all the guys can help. And we'll ask the girls at Miss Scrimmage's. If we can't come up with an idea to put this place on the map, then we don't deserve to keep Macdonald Hall!"

* * *

Elmer Drimsdale didn't want to go along on the midnight trip to Miss Scrimmage's.

"But it's against the rules! If we get caught, we'll be punished!"

"Agreed," said Bruno. "But I never get caught. Come on, Elmer, live dangerously for once in your life. We won't be punished."

"But girls make me nervous," said Elmer. "I simply cannot talk to them. My tongue dries up and my throat closes."

"Well, this is a good time to start learning," Bruno told him. He and Boots helped Elmer out the window, across the campus and over the highway. Soon Elmer was watching Bruno toss pebbles at the second-storey window.

Cathy and Diane stuck their heads out.

"We have to talk to you," called Bruno. "We're coming up."

One by one, the three boys shinnied up the drainpipe and climbed through the window.

Cathy and Diane looked at Elmer. "I see we have a newcomer," Cathy said.

"You know Elmer Drimsdale," replied Bruno.

"I've heard of you," Cathy said to Elmer. "Hi, I'm Cathy."

Elmer made a strangled noise in his throat.

"And I'm Diane." When there was no reply, Diane turned to Bruno. "Doesn't he talk?"

"Elmer's a little nervous," explained Boots. "It's something to do with his tongue and his throat. We live with Elmer now. The Fish closed Dormitory 3 and kicked us out of our room."

"That's terrible," Cathy cried. "Uh — I mean — no offence, Elmer."

"We're in big trouble," said Bruno. "The Hall is going bankrupt. It could close up soon if we don't do something. Our idea is to get some great publicity so enrolment will increase. Then there won't be any reason to close the school."

"What can we do?" asked Cathy.

"Tell the girls," Boots said. "We need ideas."

"We'll be back in a couple of days to hear what you've come up with," said Bruno. Elmer groaned. "Now, do you have any food?"

"Be right back." Diane went out quietly and was back in less than five minutes with some sandwiches. "Tomorrow's lunch," she told them.

Bruno took the bag and stuffed it into Boots's hand. He swung a leg over the window ledge and started to shinny down. Boots followed, with Elmer right behind. Bruno's feet hit the ground with a thud.

"Halt!" cried a voice.

Just as Boots slipped to the ground behind Bruno, a beam of light fell on the two of them.

At the top of the drainpipe, Elmer felt hands grasp his arms. Cathy and Diane hauled him back up over the sill and into the room.

"I *thought* I heard someone," said Miss Scrimmage. "You two should be ashamed of yourselves, coming over here and frightening my poor, innocent girls!" She pointed towards the highway. "Now, both of you, quick-march back to Macdonald Hall! I'm taking you to Mr. Sturgeon! Move!"

Miss Scrimmage grabbed their collars and marched them across the road and to the headmaster's cottage at the edge of the south lawn. Mr. Sturgeon appeared at the door in his red silk bathrobe and bedroom slippers. He took in the scene with one glance.

"Miss Scrimmage, let go of those boys this instant!" he exclaimed.

"I caught them on our grounds, frightening my poor, innocent girls. You may consider yourself lucky that I didn't turn them over to the police."

The headmaster sent Bruno and Boots into the house and placed himself between them and Miss Scrimmage. "The police," he said in icy rage, "would be interested to know how you mistreat children. Don't worry, these boys will be dealt with. Good evening." He slammed the door in her face.

When Mr. Sturgeon went inside, he found his wife comforting Bruno and Boots. "Bruno, Melvin, you poor boys! You must be awfully frightened. What were you doing over there?"

Boots held out the food parcel.

Mrs. Sturgeon opened the bag and looked inside. "Sandwiches! William, they were hungry! I told you growing boys have to have their evening snack!"

* * *

"Oh, Miss Scrimmage, it was terrible," said Cathy. "We were so scared. Thank goodness you saved us!"

Miss Scrimmage sat down on the bed where Elmer was hiding. "You poor darlings," she said. "You have nothing to fear while I am here. I can smell an intruder anywhere!"

Under the bed, some dust went up Elmer's nose. He sneezed.

"*Gezundheit,*" said Miss Scrimmage.

"Thank you," said Cathy and Diane, both at the same time.

Chapter 3

Attention, world!

At four o'clock in the morning, Bruno and Boots were awakened by a frantic scratching at the window. The two boys rushed over and pulled Elmer in.

"Where have you been?" said Bruno. "We've been worried sick!"

Elmer sat down on the floor to tell his story. "It was awful!" he moaned. "After those two girls saved me from Miss Scrimmage, they wouldn't let me leave! They made me hide under the bed! I was scared out of my mind!"

Bruno and Boots burst out laughing. Elmer was outraged. "It's not funny! I had to stay there for three hours before that Cathy person let me leave. It was the worst experience of my life!"

By this time, Bruno and Boots were laughing so hard they had collapsed to the floor.

"Go ahead and laugh, you two. You didn't have to go through what I did." Elmer glared.

"Hah!" said Boots. "Miss Scrimmage marched us to The Fish. We've got to see him in his office in the morning."

Elmer's face turned pale. "Does — does Mr. Sturgeon know about me?"

"No, you're clean," replied Boots.

Elmer sighed with relief and turned to Bruno. "You told me you never get caught."

Bruno shrugged. "It was a one-in-a-million chance," he said. "Even a pro like me can have an off night."

* * *

At exactly eight o'clock, Bruno and Boots marched through the heavy oak door with the sign saying HEADMASTER in gold letters. They sat nervously on the bench facing the desk.

Mr. Sturgeon leaned forward and fixed them with a cold, fish-like stare. "Lights-out at Macdonald Hall occurs at exactly ten o'clock," he said. "From that moment on, all students are expected to be in bed. And Miss Scrimmage's Finishing School for Young Ladies is off limits. Are these rules something new to you?"

"No, sir," Bruno said quietly.

"I'm happy to hear that. I never want to catch you over there again. Is that understood?"

"Yes, sir," said both Bruno and Boots.

"Good. I'm glad to see that you didn't involve Drimsdale in your nonsense. As for your punishment, you are to spend the rest of today in your room." He stood up. "Dismissed."

"Thank you, sir." The boys backed out of the office and hurried down the hallway.

Once outside, Boots let out a long sigh of relief. "Just one day in our room? Not bad!"

"I knew he'd go easy," replied Bruno. "He was so mad at Miss Scrimmage that he forgot he was mad at us. Anyway, we need a quiet day."

"You bet!" said Boots. "I could use a nap. I hardly slept last night."

"Who said anything about sleep?" asked Bruno. "Our suggestion box must be full by now. We have to get to work."

* * *

In Room 201, the Pacific salmon smiled down on quiet activity. Elmer's head was buried deep inside a black box that contained his latest invention, a new kind of video broadcasting machine. Bruno and Boots sat cross-legged on the floor. Between them was Boots's duffel bag, filled with small pieces of paper.

"How about this suggestion," said Boots. "*Let them close the place up so we can all go home and get a good meal. It's not signed.*"

"I'm a little disappointed," said Bruno. "The guys don't seem to have understood what we wanted. Just listen to this: *Rob a bank, get caught and get your name in the paper.* What's the matter with these idiots?"

"Here's one: *Someone should make a great discovery, like finding a cure for some terrible disease.*"

"That's Elmer's job," laughed Bruno. "Hey, Elm, as soon as you're finished with that TV thing, would you mind discovering a cure for some dread disease?"

Elmer lifted his head from the black box. "Of course," he said seriously. "I'm already working on a cure for the common cold."

"I thought you were working on that TV thing," said Boots.

"That too," replied Elmer. "I'm currently involved in seventeen projects — or is it eighteen? I don't remember." His head disappeared again.

Boots cast Bruno a look of wonder. "Does he ever finish anything?"

"At last!" cried Elmer. "It's finished!" He leaped to his feet. "Would you mind helping me set it up to test it?"

"Sure," said Bruno.

Elmer began gathering equipment from every corner of the room. Bruno and Boots spent the next hour finding and holding electronic gear for him as he set up his invention. When it was all done, odds and ends of wires and electrical parts were connected to the black box. So were a camera and a microphone. The lens of the camera pointed at Elmer's Pacific salmon poster. On the black box was a small TV screen and speaker.

"Now we try it out," said Elmer. "The salmon should appear on the screen and whatever we say will come out of the speaker."

He reached for the *On* switch.

* * *

"Isn't this movie exciting, William?" said Mrs. Sturgeon. "How do you think it will end?"

"We'll know soon enough, Mildred," replied Mr. Sturgeon. "It'll be over in five minutes."

Suddenly, there was a buzz of static and the screen went blank. The movie was replaced by the fuzzy image of a large fish. The audio crackled, and a garbled voice cried, *"Attention, world! We bring you the Fish!"* This was followed by what sounded like laughter.

Mr. Sturgeon frowned. "A fish. How strange."

"But why is it there?" asked Mrs. Sturgeon.

Both stared at the screen until the image of the fish faded out. It was replaced by the words *The End*.

* * *

"Wow, Elmer, it works!" cried Bruno, jumping up and down in the small space left in the room.

"It's fantastic!" said Boots.

"Yes," agreed Elmer. "It would seem that I am on the right track."

"Hey, I know!" said Bruno. "We can use this thing to get on people's TV sets and tell them how great Macdonald Hall is."

"No, no," Elmer smiled. "It will only broadcast to the screen and speaker on my black box. It will take me a few more months to make it broadcast the way you want."

What Elmer didn't know was that everyone watching TV within thirty kilometres was wondering why "the Fish" had invaded their homes.

Chapter 4

We're looking into it

In her five years as weekend telephone operator at CHUT-TV, Mary Webster had never had such a busy time as on that Sunday afternoon.

"Every caller wants to know what happened at the end of the movie," she told her boss, Mr. Tupper. "They're all telling me something about a fish."

Mr. Tupper frowned. "A fish? What about a fish?"

"It appeared at the end of the movie. The screen showed a big fish. Then someone said, 'Attention, world! We bring you the Fish.' Then there was the most evil laughter. It really scared some of our viewers."

"Sounds like a message from outer space," laughed Mr. Tupper. "The invasion of the Fish People. Just make up something about weather effects and tell people we're looking into it."

* * *

Elmer's alarm went off at six o'clock Monday morning. He threw off the covers and leaped out of bed. He breathed deeply, but couldn't do his morning exercises. There was no space.

"The beginning of another day!" he announced cheerfully. "Time to tend all my little friends."

A slipper flew past his ear. "Your little friends will be fine. It's your big friends you've got to worry about," growled Bruno.

Boots sneezed five times, the signal that he was awake for the day. He slowly crawled out of bed.

"Would you like to feed my goldfish?" Elmer offered.

"No, thanks," said Boots. "Maybe some other time."

"Would you like to sprinkle a little sugar for my ant colony?"

"Oh, all right," sighed Boots. He took the sugar box over to the ant colony, removed the cover and switched on the lamp. He sprinkled a little sugar on top of the sand, and a dozen ants appeared. "Hey, Bruno," he shouted, "you should see this. A mini riot!" Bruno didn't move.

At 7:15, Boots and Elmer left for the dining hall. Bruno hopped out of bed and went to Elmer's video machine. He switched it on and watched as the salmon appeared on the screen.

"The Fish has arisen," he said in the deepest voice he could. *"The Fish is everywhere. Beware the Fish!"* He laughed with glee and switched off the machine.

Bruno sighed. It was too bad Elmer's machine couldn't send signals to anything but the little screen on the black box. Bruno would have loved to broadcast his fish jokes to Mr. Sturgeon's TV. The headmaster would never know it was him.

But Bruno's message had already reached Mr. Sturgeon. Like every other TV viewer near Macdonald Hall, he saw Elmer's salmon during the CHUT-TV *Early Show.*

* * *

It was after four when Bruno and Boots made their way back to Room 201. When they opened the door, they were greeted by an amazing sight. Elmer had set up a large chemistry lab. The table was covered with pieces of equipment of all shapes and sizes.

"Elmer, what's going on?" asked Bruno.

"My cure for the common cold. I think I'm on the right track," replied Elmer.

"But we have to live here!" cried Boots.

"Do you know how much publicity a cure for the common cold would bring to Macdonald Hall?" asked Bruno. "You go ahead and work, Elm. Take all the room you need!"

"Thank you," mumbled Elmer.

Bruno climbed across Boots's bed and worked his way over to his favourite invention. He switched it on and waited for the fish image to appear on the screen.

"This is the Fish Patrol," he said loudly. "We bring you greetings from the fishbowl." He added an evil laugh. "Beware the Fish! You never know where he may strike next." Bruno switched off the machine. "Great!"

"You'd better hope The Fish never hears all that," noted Boots.

"How can he hear it? We're our own little TV station," laughed Bruno.

But in the headmaster's home, a fed-up Mrs. Sturgeon was dialling CHUT-TV.

* * *

"What suggestions did you get for making the Hall famous?" asked Boots. It was midnight and he and Bruno were visiting the girls.

"Most of the ideas we got were pretty stupid," said Cathy. "Rob a bank and stuff like that, so you'll get your names in the paper."

"We got a lot of that from the guys too," Bruno muttered. "Don't tell me that's the best you can do."

"No problem," she said brightly. "I, Catherine Elizabeth Burton, have thought up the solution to your problem. You guys just have to set a world record at something and get Macdonald Hall into the *Rankin Book of World Records*."

"That's a great idea!" cried Bruno. "We've got so much talent at the Hall, it'll be easy. Let's go get started."

Bruno swung himself over the sill and shinnied down the pipe. Boots started to follow, when suddenly they heard an all-too-familiar voice.

"Halt!"

The two girls ran to the window and looked out. Bruno was lit up in the beam of Miss Scrimmage's flashlight. Boots was clinging to the pipe part way down.

"What'll we do?" whispered Diane.

"I know. I'll create a diversion." Cathy burst into loud screaming.

Startled, Boots lost his grip on the drainpipe. He fell a full two metres and landed on Miss Scrimmage. Her flashlight flew into the air.

Boots jumped to his feet and ran, leaving Miss Scrimmage screaming, "Assault! Assault!" Bruno took off after him, and they didn't stop until they were safe in Room 201.

Bruno was the first to find his voice. "I don't believe it! She did it again! She caught me! *Me!* Who does she think she is?"

"Are you going to be punished?" asked Elmer.

"No," said Bruno.

"Yes," said Boots.

"Either way," said Bruno, "we've got a lot of work ahead of us. A world record, remember?"

"We might have one already," snapped Boots. "Most times caught by a crazy headmistress."

"Don't rub it in," moaned Bruno. "I've suffered enough." He walked over to Elmer's video machine.

Chapter 5

A brainwave

"Men," said Bruno at lunch, "I now call upon you all to save Macdonald Hall. We've decided on the best way to become famous. We have to get ourselves into the *Rankin Book of World Records*." He slammed a thick book onto his tray. "All we have to do is take a record and beat it. Who's game?" There was total silence.

Boots opened the book. "We'd like to save the school," he sighed, "but world records are hard to break. Look at this. The record for riding a Ferris wheel is more than four weeks! I can't see me asking The Fish for four weeks off school for something like that!"

Bruno flipped a couple of pages. "Hey, this is it! A tin-can pyramid! The record is a pyramid with a base 2.4 metres square. It was 4.6 metres high and used 22 140 pop cans. The base was forty cans by forty cans. We'll make one with a base forty-five cans square. Elmer?"

Elmer chewed on a dried fig. "That would require 31 395 cans."

"No sweat!" exclaimed Bruno. "Everywhere you look there are pop cans lying around."

"In this case," said Boots, "the litterbug is our best friend."

"If we can get everyone in the school looking for pop cans, I'm sure we'll find enough. We can get the girls at Scrimmage's to help too."

"We'd have to go off campus," warned Boots. "We can't have everyone asking for leave on the same day. I take it we don't want The Fish to know about this."

"The way I see it," said Bruno, "we can all walk to Chutney on Friday night. From there, we can catch buses to all over the place. Somebody can even go to Toronto. We'll all come back sometime Saturday."

There were wild shouts of protest.

Bruno stood up and pounded the table. "All right, you guys, I know it's dangerous. But The Fish won't be able to expel all six hundred of us. If we don't do it, we might as well go home, because pretty soon there won't be any Macdonald Hall."

* * *

"What's happening with the world records?" asked Cathy.

"Plenty," replied Boots. "Bruno's got the whole school in an uproar over it."

"Terrific," exclaimed Cathy. "I love uproars. Can we help?"

"As a matter of fact, you can," said Bruno. "We're going for the world's largest pop-can pyramid. We need some cans."

"How many?" asked Diane.

"Oh, no more than 32 000," said Bruno.

"Yeah, right," said Cathy. "No problem. Tomorrow, I'll just stroll out and pick up 32 000 pop cans."

"Listen," insisted Bruno. "Just tell the girls to get all the pop cans they can find."

"You've picked a good time. The whole school is going to the Art Gallery of Ontario in Toronto on Saturday — or so Miss Scrimmage thinks."

"Cathy!" Diane protested. "We can't —"

"We can and we will," was Cathy's reply. "And Miss Scrimmage can't expel us because we're taking the whole school along. There's strength in numbers."

Boots gave Bruno a strange look. He had heard that before.

"Great," said Bruno, swinging his foot over the window sill. "See you."

He shinnied down the pipe and waited for Boots to catch up. As Boots landed beside him, a voice cried, "Halt!"

"Oh, no!" moaned Bruno. "It's Miss Scrimmage again. What does she *want* from me?"

"Your neck," snapped Boots. "And mine. Let's go!"

The two boys took off towards Macdonald Hall at a dead run.

* * *

Elmer pulled Bruno and Boots in through the window of Room 201. "Where have you been? It's after three!"

Bruno cast Elmer a look that could have melted lead. He hurled himself onto his bed without a word.

"You'll have to excuse him," Boots explained with a grin. "Miss Scrimmage nearly caught us again. He's having a confidence crisis."

"I don't know," Bruno growled. "It's getting to be so a guy can't sneak out after lights-out anymore. What's going on here anyway?"

Boots shrugged and started to get ready for bed.

"I have some news," offered Elmer. "My cure for the common cold is ready to be tested."

"Wow!" said Bruno. "We'll do that tomorrow! Who do we know with a cold?"

"Nobody right now," said Boots. "It's not the cold season."

"Surely *somebody* has a cold," insisted Bruno.

Across the hall in Room 200, Coach Flynn went into a fit of sneezing. He could be heard rustling around, clearing his throat and blowing his nose.

Bruno and Boots exchanged looks of pure delight.

Chapter 6

An uncommon cure

"And that's how I expect you to complete the obstacle course," said Coach Flynn, jumping off the climbing equipment in the gym. "Any questions?" He sneezed violently.

Bruno elbowed Boots. Boots raised his hand.

"Sir, isn't there too much space between the vaulting horse and the springboard? Could we take a closer look?"

While Flynn and the rest of the class checked it out, Bruno stole over to the bench where the coach had set his glass of Muscle-Ade, the high-energy drink he always used. From the pocket of his shorts, Bruno took out the eye-dropper bottle of cold remedy Elmer had given him. Holding the dropper over the coach's glass, he put in exactly six drops. Then he strolled back and merged with the group.

The coach sneezed again. "Oh, this cold!" he groaned.

"Maybe some Muscle-Ade will help," suggested Bruno. "People with colds should drink a lot."

"Good idea," agreed Flynn. He jogged over to the bench, picked up his glass and drained it.

Boots shut his eyes.

A puzzled look came over Flynn's face.

"Strange," he said. "It never tasted like this before." He hiccupped, took three steps and collapsed to the floor, where he began to snore loudly. Between snores, he continued to hiccup.

Boots opened his eyes and took in the scene with a gasp of horror. "Bruno, look what we did!"

"He'll be all right," declared Bruno. "He's just asleep. Funny Elmer didn't mention that he was going to fall asleep. It must be some kind of reaction."

"What happened?" cried Pete Anderson. "I'd better go get The Fish!"

"No! No Fish!" shouted Bruno. "No Fish!"

"Fish," murmured Flynn sleepily. A goofy grin spread over his face. He raised his head and tried to open his eyes. Then he flopped back down.

"What'll we do?" asked Pete nervously.

"We'd better take him home to bed," Bruno decided.

"How are we going to do that without anyone noticing?" demanded Boots.

"If we all crowd around him," explained Bruno, "we can walk him there." He looked at the rest of the class. "You guys with us?"

"Let's get him out of here!" said someone.

Bruno and Boots lifted their coach to his feet. The boys crowded around them, and together they walked him towards Dormitory 2. Coach Flynn hiccupped all the way.

"Open the door!" panted Boots.

Bruno plucked the key from Flynn's jacket pocket and unlocked the door. Then he and Boots dragged the coach across the room and dropped him onto his bed.

"Paper," ordered Bruno. "Get paper."

"We don't need paper! We need an ambulance!" cried Boots.

"We've got to put a sign on the gym door saying afternoon classes are cancelled."

"But, Bruno, what if — "

"Just get me the paper. When we finish the sign, we'll go find Elmer."

"All right, guys," mumbled Flynn. "Everybody onto the obstacle course. Speed it up." He ended with another loud hiccup.

Boots shot Bruno a worried look as they left the room. "Even if Elmer's cure really works, it may be worse than the disease," he muttered.

Bruno and Boots caught up with Elmer at the entrance to the dining hall.

"Elmer, we have to talk to you!" said Bruno.

"Your stupid cold cure!" cried Boots. "It poisoned the coach!"

"Impossible," said Elmer. "There is no toxic material in my formula."

"Then why did he pass out?" cried Boots.

Elmer cocked his head. "He shouldn't have. Perhaps it's all in his mind. Did you tell him that it's harmless?"

"Not exactly," replied Bruno. "We slipped it into his Muscle-Ade."

"Oh, dear!" said Elmer. "Muscle-Ade has lemon juice in it. My formula should never be taken with lemon juice."

"What happens?" gasped Boots.

"There is a reaction," explained Elmer. "First, the diaphragm contracts. The diaphragm, of course, is the muscle and tendons that separate the chest from the abdomen. Then, the central nervous system — "

"Elmer, speak English!" Bruno snapped.

"It gives you the hiccups and makes you very sleepy," said Elmer. "Sometimes, it even leads to sleepwalking."

"Oh, no!" moaned Boots. "How long does all this last?"

"Just a few hours. But it will never do for anyone to see him in this condition. Perhaps you should watch him until the effects wear off," suggested Elmer. "After all, it is your fault."

"*Our* fault?" objected Bruno as they headed back to Dormitory 2. "It's *your* cure!"

"It was given incorrectly," accused Elmer. "If you wanted to cure his cold, you should have asked me how to use it."

When they got to Room 200, the door was open. Flynn was gone.

"Oh, no!" moaned Boots. "Where can he be?"

47

"If you were a sleepwalking gym teacher with the hiccups, where would you go?" asked Bruno.

"I would stay home where I wouldn't worry my students!" muttered Boots.

The three boys ran out of Dormitory 2 and were about to go searching when, from across the road, Miss Scrimmage's outdoor public address system sprang to life.

A loud hiccup rang out over the campus. Then a male voice mumbled sleepily, *"Good work, guys. That's it for the obstacle course."*

A voice they recognized as Cathy Burton's broke in. *"We have a stray here,"* she said. In the background, the boys heard another huge hiccup. *"He's tall, red-haired, and answers to the name of Al. Would someone please come to claim him."*

Chapter 7

Operation Pop Can

After lights-out on Friday night, the woods behind Macdonald Hall was crawling with boys setting out on the great pop-can roundup.

Bruno and Boots caught up with Larry Wilson. "How come you're going, Larry?" asked Bruno. "What if The Fish needs a messenger tomorrow and you're not back yet?"

"I'm just going as far as the movie theatre outside Chutney," Larry replied. "Pete's already there. I'll take his cans home and he'll go on from there." He squinted in the dark. "Say, where's Elmer?"

"He's staying home," explained Boots. "He's working on some remote-control thingamajig."

"Where are you guys going?" asked Larry.

"To Toronto." Bruno made it sound easy.

As usual, Boots was worried. "Bruno, Toronto is awfully far. I thought we'd just sort of hang around Chutney."

"If all of us just hang around Chutney," pointed out Bruno, "we won't get enough cans, will we?"

* * *

Just before dawn, a group of fifteen boys crept back onto the Macdonald Hall campus, each carrying a large bag full of cans. They sneaked across the lawn to the abandoned Dormitory 3 and opened the main door.

Pete Anderson stepped inside. "Wow!" he whispered admiringly. "Look at this!"

The dormitory hall was lined with neatly stacked pop cans, already stretching past two doorways. The stacks were four cans high.

"We'll have to stack ours too," Pete whispered to the other boys. "That's what everyone else is doing." To set a good example, he began placing his cans one by one in a neat stack with the others.

Their cans all neatly stowed away, the boys headed for their rooms to catch two hours of sleep before breakfast.

* * *

Dawn found Bruno Walton and Boots O'Neal in Toronto's High Park. As Bruno put it, "High Park is right in the middle of a city. There are picnics, school field trips, office workers having lunch — there must be millions of pop cans!"

And there were. The recycling bins were piled high with the previous day's leavings. The city cleanup crew hadn't come on duty yet.

"We should have brought more guys!" exclaimed Bruno. "We could get 32 000 cans just from this park!"

"Who else would be stupid enough to come all the way to Toronto?" moaned Boots, yawning. "How are we going to get all these cans back to the Hall?"

"That's the easy part," said Bruno, "as long as we get to the Art Gallery by four o'clock."

"Scrimmage's trip?" asked Boots.

"They're going to have two or three buses," Bruno explained. "Surely they'll have room for little old us."

"Bruno, we've got two huge bags of junk apiece! Do you really think we can just slip onto one of their buses unnoticed?"

"The girls will all have big bags of junk too," said Bruno. "Don't worry. I'll look after everything."

"I'd rather take the bus to Chutney and walk back to the Hall," Boots replied.

"Well, let me put it this way," said Bruno. "We have enough money for bus fare or for lunch. Take your choice."

* * *

Outside the Art Gallery, Miss Scrimmage's girls were getting ready to leave. Dragging their clanking bags, Bruno and Boots merged with the crowd.

Miss Scrimmage stood at the door of one of the buses. "My goodness," she said, "why is everyone carrying such huge parcels?"

"Souvenirs," said Cathy.

"Oh, how nice!" exclaimed the headmistress with delight. "I *am* pleased that you all enjoyed the gallery. Let me have a peek." She looked into the bag of the first girl in line. "Uh — splendid," she said, with a puzzled look on her face. "All right now, girls, everyone on the buses."

They all climbed on. Bruno and Boots kept their heads down and stayed hidden in the crowd. When they sat down, Cathy and Diane found a seat in front of them. Miss Scrimmage rode in the seat behind the driver.

When the buses finally pulled into the school driveway, Bruno leaned over and tapped Cathy on the shoulder.

"You'll have to take our stuff," he said. "We'll never get across the road with it now. Leave everything in the orchard. We'll come over to pick it up tonight around midnight. Come on, Boots. We'll go out the emergency exit."

"But —" Diane protested.

She was too late. As Bruno pulled the lever, a loud buzzer sounded. Bruno grabbed Boots, and the two shot off across the road.

"Who did that?" called Miss Scrimmage.

"The door must be broken," Cathy called back. "It's a good thing nobody fell out on the way home."

"Quite right," said Miss Scrimmage. "I shall complain to the bus company."

* * *

"I'm glad to see we're all present and accounted for," said Bruno at the dinner table that night.

Immediately, complaints about the dangers and discomforts of the hunt filled the air. They were all directed at Bruno Walton.

"But did you get lots of cans?" cried Bruno over the noise.

"When you see Dormitory 3," said Pete, "you'll freak out! I didn't think there were that many cans in the world!"

"The girls got a lot too," said Boots. "They've hidden them in the apple orchard."

"We're going to get them tonight," Bruno added.

"When are we going to build the pyramid?" asked Boots.

"Next Saturday," Bruno said. "I've already called the TV station in Chutney to come and witness it for us."

"We're going to be on TV?"

"Yes," said Bruno with great satisfaction. "*The Rankin Book of World Records* and publicity too!"

Chapter 8

A question of ownership

Cathy Burton and Diane Grant were standing at their window watching as twenty-five Macdonald Hall students climbed over the fence. It took only a few minutes for the boys to find the pop cans the girls had hidden in the apple orchard.

They gathered the bags and began to move silently back towards Macdonald Hall. In the lead, Bruno and Boots were just about to step onto the highway.

"Halt!"

"Run!" bellowed Bruno, and twenty-five yelling boys thundered across the road. Miss Scrimmage ran after them, followed by a stream of girls dressed in night clothes.

"No!" howled Bruno, seeing his crew heading for Dormitory 3. "Don't lead her there!" He couldn't be heard over the general noise. "No! Stop!" He ran after them.

"Stop, thieves!" screeched Miss Scrimmage, still running at the head of her army of girls.

The boys arrived at Dormitory 3, threw open the door and rushed inside. They dropped their bags, kicking the neatly stacked pop cans all over the hall. One of the boys fell, starting a chain reaction. Soon all twenty-five boys were down on the floor. More boys poured in through the doorway, all tripping and tumbling.

"What's going on?"

"Our pop cans!"

Outside, an angry Miss Scrimmage was being held back by some of the girls.

"Don't go in there, Miss Scrimmage," Diane Grant pleaded. "You won't like it!"

"Release me!" insisted Miss Scrimmage.

Bruno scrambled out through the door of Dormitory 3.

"There's one of them!" cried Miss Scrimmage. "Stop, thief!" She pulled herself loose and began to chase Bruno around the building. A crowd of her girls followed, screaming for her to come back. Boots darted after them.

Bruno gulped as he ran. Rushing towards him was a figure in a red silk bathrobe and bedroom slippers. It was Mr. Sturgeon.

"Hello, sir," panted Bruno as they met.

The headmaster thrust Bruno behind him, held up both hands and said quietly and firmly, "Stop this *at once!*"

Boots ran up and joined Bruno behind Mr. Sturgeon.

"Proof at last!" cried Miss Scrimmage. "Your boys robbed our school and stashed the loot in there! Have a look!"

"I believe I will," responded a grim-faced Mr. Sturgeon. He walked around the corner of the building to the front door of Dormitory 3 and looked inside. His jaw dropped in amazement. About fifty of his students were inside, swimming in a sea of pop cans.

Mr. Sturgeon turned to Miss Scrimmage. "Nothing has been stolen from your school, I assure you. Now, would you and your girls please leave."

Miss Scrimmage gathered up her students and began to march towards home.

Mr. Sturgeon turned to his boys. "You will all go to your beds now." The boys began to scatter. "Walton, O'Neal, not you two. I will see you in my office."

Silently, Bruno and Boots followed the headmaster into his office. They seated themselves on the bench.

Mr. Sturgeon closed the door and began pacing in front of them. "Now," he said grimly, "I want an explanation. From the beginning."

"Well, sir," began Bruno. There seemed no way out of it, and he was about to resort to the truth. "It's like this. We were —"

Suddenly there was the sound of running feet in the hall outside. The door flew open and in burst Cathy Burton.

"Oh, sir," she panted, "I confess! The pop cans — they're mine!"

"Cathy —"

"Silence!" thundered Mr. Sturgeon. "You are Miss Burton, I believe. Tell me, Miss Burton, how did you get so many soft-drink cans?"

"I'm a collector, sir," Cathy explained. "I can never pass up a pop can. When I see one, I just have to have it. I now have 41 683. It's one of the biggest collections in the country," she said proudly. "But it was clogging my room. So I talked Bruno and Boots into letting me keep the cans in your empty dormitory. It was all my fault, sir. I'm sorry."

Mr. Sturgeon had a long coughing spell. Finally, he asked, "Does Miss Scrimmage know about your famous collection?"

"Uh — no, sir," replied Cathy.

"Well," said the headmaster, "why don't we tell her?" He reached for the telephone.

"Hello, Miss Scrimmage. I think I have straightened things out around here. There is a Miss Burton in my office at the moment . . . No, she is here of her own free will. We have not kidnapped her . . . She is here to confess to the ownership of 41 683 pop cans, which are now in my dormitory. Isn't that right, Miss Burton?"

"Yes, sir," mumbled Cathy.

"They belong to her," Mr. Sturgeon continued, "and therefore to you. I'm sure that you will want to claim them for your school. So

I expect them — all of them — to be out of my dormitory by noon tomorrow. I shall escort Miss Burton home. Goodnight."

Mr. Sturgeon hung up the phone. "Off to bed, boys. Come along, Miss Burton. I'll take you home."

Chapter 9

A little accident

Bruno Walton crawled out of bed late on Sunday morning. He went over to Elmer's video machine and flicked the *On* button. *"Be warned,"* he said in a deep voice. *"The Fish will have revenge."*

"Bruno, why do you keep doing that?" asked Boots. "You know no one can hear it."

"It makes me feel better," said Bruno. "Miss Scrimmage is driving me crazy." He wandered over to the window and lifted the blind. "Will you look at that!"

A long line of girls stretched from Dormitory 3 all the way across the road to Miss Scrimmage's. At the door of the dormitory stood the headmistress herself, supervising the removal of the pop cans.

The door opened. Elmer climbed in over Boots's bed and made his way towards his newest project. "Good morning," he said. "I was just down the hall getting some parts from an old VCR."

"Great," said Bruno. Elmer was working on a new discovery — a high-speed remote-control device — and Bruno was doing everything he could to help. It was another chance for publicity! "You get to work," he added. "Boots and I will take care of your plants and stuff."

"Yeah, I'll do the ants," offered Boots. "Ants are my specialty."

* * *

At lunch time, Larry Wilson came tearing into the dining hall. "We've got trouble!" he said. "I just heard that on Saturday, a big real estate developer is coming out here. He wants to buy the Hall and tear it down to build apartments!"

"So, it's started," Bruno groaned. "It's the beginning of the end." He pounded the table. "But it's not too late! We've lost a battle, but the war's not over yet! People with a good cause don't give up! We're going to convince that real estate developer that this is the last place anybody would want to build!"

He sat down amid wild clapping. Boots wasn't usually affected by Bruno's acting, but even he was moved. "That was great, Bruno!" he exclaimed. "So how are we going to get rid of the developer?"

"I'll think of something later," whispered Bruno under cover of the general noise.

A group of boys hoisted Bruno to their shoulders and carried him around the campus in a snake dance. A cheering crowd followed.

"But he has no plan!" said Boots to thin air.

* * *

Boots looked up from his homework. "Bruno, how can you just sit there?" he asked. "You got everybody all worked up and you don't even have a plan! What are we going to do?"

"I'll think of something," replied Bruno.

Music from across the road wafted in through the open window.

"Pretty good," murmured Boots.

"What?" asked Bruno.

"Scrimmage's band. They're pretty good, don't you think?"

"They're a little loud," said Elmer. "After all, we do have work to do here."

Bruno's face took on a thoughtful look. "But what if they were *bad*? And *very* loud? Who would want to live across the street from that? Who would want to build here then?"

"Bruno, what are you saying?" asked Boots.

Bruno tossed his math book into a pile of laundry. "I'm saying that by Saturday, with our help, Miss Scrimmage's band is going to get a lot bigger, a lot louder and a lot worse! That developer is going to head for the hills when he sees — and hears — what's across the road from his apartment building-to-be! Or not-to-be!"

"Bruno, we'll get expelled!"

"Nobody will see us," returned Bruno. "Mr. Sturgeon won't be here. He and the staff are going to a Board meeting."

* * *

Saturday lunch was just drawing to a close at Miss Scrimmage's. Cathy Burton got to her feet. She tapped a spoon against her water glass for attention.

"All right, girls," she announced, "we're having a special kind of band practice today. I want the whole school on the front lawn in fifteen minutes. Everyone bring something to play. That includes kazoos, harmonicas and whistles. If you don't have anything else, bring a spoon and a garbage-can lid to bang on."

"What's this all about?" asked someone.

"Macdonald Hall is coming over," Cathy replied with a grin. "We're going to update the big-band sound."

In fifteen minutes, the lawn in front of Miss Scrimmage's Finishing School for Young Ladies was packed with people. Cathy had brought out a microphone for Miss Scrimmage's PA system.

"Wow, we're going to blast that developer away!" exclaimed Bruno with glee.

"We're certainly going to try," Cathy agreed. "Let's start!"

"No, no, no," begged Boots, tuning his guitar. "Let's wait till the developer gets here. If we start too soon, Miss Scrimmage will catch us."

"She's not here," said Cathy. "She went out to the beauty shop for a checkup."

Bruno laughed and turned to Elmer. "Hey, Elm, what are you playing?"

"Well," began Elmer, "I thought I'd just listen and —"

"What do you mean 'just listen'?" Cathy cried. "Everybody has to take part!" She stuffed the microphone into his hands. "You can be the lead singer!"

"I don't sing," protested Elmer weakly.

"Learn," said Cathy.

"There's a car coming! It must be the developer!" bellowed Bruno.

"This is it!" shouted Cathy. "And-a-one, and-a-two, and-a-one-two-three!"

The band exploded into a riot of noise. Trumpets blared and garbage cans clanged. The effect was awful.

Cathy poked Elmer. "You're not singing."

Elmer grabbed the mike, shut his eyes and began to shout the only thing he knew — science facts. "The area of a circle equals *pi* times the square of the radius," he howled.

Bruno, who had been blowing through a vacuum cleaner hose, broke into wild laughter.

"A floating object displaces its own weight in liquid," sang Elmer. "The kangaroo is a marsupial. Yes! Oh, yes!"

A truck pulled up and parked across the road. On the side, in red block letters, was written CHUT-TV.

"Oh, no!" Bruno shouted at Boots. "I forgot to call them off!"

Two men got out of the truck. They held their ears and scanned the Macdonald Hall campus. Seeing no one there, they crossed the road towards the huge band.

One of the men shouted, "Do any of you kids know where the world's largest tin-can pyramid is?"

"Never heard of it," said Bruno quickly.

"Any of you know this guy Walton who phoned us?"

"Never heard of him either," said Bruno.

"You know," said the other man, "we have to get some kind of story. Why don't we do one on these kids? What do you call yourselves?"

Cathy stepped forward. "This is Elmer Dynamite and the Original Round-Robin

Happy-Go-Lucky Heel-Clicking Foot-Stomping Beat-Swinging Scrim-Band."

"How about doing a number?" the first man asked. "Get this Dynamite guy up front."

As the camera recorded, Elmer began to sing again. "Geometry," he bawled. "The square of the hypotenuse . . ."

"Keep playing," Bruno told the others. "There's a car coming. It must be the developer."

A limousine pulled up and parked in front of Macdonald Hall. Out stepped the developer, a short man in a grey suit. He held his ears and made a face. The band played louder.

"The sine of any angle equals the cosine of its complement," shrieked Elmer.

The developer approached, waving his arms for silence. The din faded.

"Hello, sir," said Bruno with a wide, toothy grin. "Can we help you?"

The man looked sick. "Do you do this often?"

"Three times a day," said Bruno cheerfully.

"Mostly at night," Cathy added.

"We're usually louder," added Bruno, "but a lot of the kids are away for the day."

"Listen to how good we are!" yelled Cathy. "One, two, three —" The band erupted once more, with Elmer shouting about dinosaurs.

Down the highway rolled a black pickup truck. Miss Scrimmage's head was hanging out the window. She was staring and shouting, but no one could hear her over the noise of the band.

Crash! The pickup ploughed into the limousine. The music died abruptly.

"Oh, no!" moaned Boots in the silence.

"Are you crazy, lady?" bellowed the developer. The front of his limousine was mangled. The radiator was spewing water, the hood was crumpled like an accordion, and the windshield was smashed.

Dropping their instruments, Miss Scrimmage's girls rushed to her rescue.

"I'm perfectly all right," she told them. "It was only a little accident."

"A little accident!" screamed the developer. "That was a seventy-thousand-dollar car!"

"None of the children was hurt, and that's the main thing," declared Miss Scrimmage.

Chapter 10

But will it fly?

"Bruno, what are you moping about?" asked Boots. "We got rid of the developer, didn't we?"

"Yeah," said Bruno. "But he'll be back. I guess we were pretty stupid to think that a little noise would drive a guy away from a multi-million-dollar real estate deal."

Elmer interrupted. "It's ready," he said.

"What's ready?" asked Bruno.

"My remote-control device," said Elmer. "It's ready for testing."

"All right!" cried Bruno, jumping to his feet. "Another chance to be famous! How do we go about testing it?"

"We take it outdoors and fly it," said Elmer.

"Okay, let's do it right now. Where's the best place?"

"Actually, the only place to test it properly is in an area where there are trees. Then I can see how well it handles and how well the signal travels."

"Scrimmage's apple orchard," decided Bruno. "It's perfect."

"Yes, it would be ideal," Elmer agreed. "However, I strongly doubt that Mr. Sturgeon or Miss Scrimmage would grant permission."

"True," agreed Bruno, "but they can't object if they don't know about it."

"No," said Boots simply, "we're not going there again."

"Don't be silly!" scoffed Bruno. "Miss Scrimmage guards her students, not her apples. We'll go tonight."

Elmer protested. "I'm not sure I want to —"

"What a pair of chickens!" interrupted Bruno. "The matter is settled." To make his point, he switched on Elmer's video machine. "*Greetings once more from the Fish Patrol,*" he began.

* * *

Mr. Sturgeon switched on the television set to watch the ten o'clock news. The announcer appeared on screen, smiled, opened his mouth to speak — and vanished. Once again, the image of a fish showed up. Then a voice said, "*Greetings once more from the Fish Patrol. Operation Flying Fish will start tonight at midnight. You never know when the Fish may descend on you. Beware the Fish!*"

"Mildred," said Mr. Sturgeon to his wife, "I'm sure I know that voice. I just can't place it."

* * *

The midnight quiet was disturbed as three dark figures eased over the fence and crept into the cover of the apple orchard.

"Here's a good spot," said Bruno, dropping his burden.

Elmer nodded, too frightened to speak.

Boots was nervous too. "Any sign of Miss Scrimmage?"

Bruno didn't reply. "Okay, Elmer, set it up."

In fifteen minutes, Elmer had assembled a large box covered with buttons and topped by a tall antenna. In his hand, he held a metal ball studded with Christmas-tree lights. He flicked a switch to turn the machine on and placed the ball inside a black tube attached to the box.

"Wait!" said Bruno suddenly. He pulled the ball out of the tube. "It's bad luck to launch a ship without a name." With a marker, he carefully printed M.H.*Flying Fish* on a clear patch of metal.

"M.H.?" questioned Boots.

"Macdonald Hall, of course," said Bruno. He returned the little craft to the tube. "And now for the test."

Elmer flicked another switch and turned a dial. There was a clunk, and the M.H.*Flying Fish* shot out of the tube. It hovered among the branches of the trees, humming as it waited for instructions.

"Terrific!" cheered Bruno as he and Boots stared at the ball. It lit up the area where they stood.

Skilfully, Elmer worked the controls to move the craft in, around and over the trees.

Suddenly, there was a rustling in the darkness behind them. A voice called, "Halt!"

The three boys wheeled in horror.

Cathy Burton appeared from behind a tree. "Just kidding," she said. She grinned and glanced behind her. "Come on out, Diane. I told you it was them."

Diane appeared at her side. "What are you guys doing? What is that thing?"

"It's our ship," replied Bruno. "Elmer will explain it to you."

Elmer shook his head, unable to speak in the presence of the girls.

"Oh, it's Elmer!" said Cathy. She strode over to the console. "Hey, cool! What does this thing do?" She grasped one of the dials and twisted it as far as it would go.

"No!" cried Elmer.

The M.H. *Flying Fish* shot up and away into the sky. Elmer quickly hit some buttons, but it was too late. The lights could no longer be seen.

"Our ship!" cried Bruno. "Bring it back!"

"I can't," said Elmer sadly. "I'm afraid it's out of range."

"Oops," said Cathy. "Sorry."

"*Cath-y!*" moaned Bruno. "That was going to make us famous and you lost it!"

"Sorry," repeated Cathy. "Maybe you can build another one."

"I want to go home," said Elmer.

"Yeah," agreed Boots. "Let's get out of here."

The three boys picked up their equipment and turned to go.

"Intruders, halt!" shrieked a voice in the distance.

"A perfect ending to a perfect evening!" muttered Boots.

"Here she comes again," agreed Cathy. "You guys get going."

"What about you?" asked Bruno.

"Oh, don't worry about us," said Cathy. "If she catches us, we'll just tell her you've been bothering us again."

* * *

The boys climbed back through the window and flopped on their beds. "Another plan down the drain," Bruno groaned. "That Cathy! Why did she have to go and do that!"

"It was just an accident, Bruno," argued Boots protectively. "She didn't mean it."

"It was also a flaw in my thinking," admitted Elmer. "Because of the speed of the craft, I should have expanded the range of the controls." He sighed. "It was out of range in less than three seconds."

"Still," snapped Bruno, "if it hadn't been for her . . ."

Chapter 11

The Fish suspects

"This is the Fish Patrol in 201," came the voice. *"Our Flying Fish flew away. But we'll fight to the bitter end! Beware the Fish!"*

Mr. Sturgeon grasped the arms of his chair and sat bolt upright. "201," he repeated. "2-0-1! Walton!"

* * *

"Have I done anything lately?" asked Bruno.

Larry Wilson had just given him a message from the headmaster. Bruno was to report to Mr. Sturgeon's house.

"What kind of a question is that?" demanded Boots nervously. "We've all done quite a lot lately!"

A little worried, Bruno jogged across the campus. He had never been ordered to the headmaster's home before. He approached the door nervously and rang the bell.

Mr. Sturgeon opened the door and fixed his visitor with the coldest of fishy stares.

"You sent for me, sir?"

"I did," replied the headmaster grimly. "Uh — sit down, Walton." Then he paused, as if he wasn't sure what to say next.

"Yes, sir?" Bruno prompted.

"Lately," the headmaster began, "a lot of strange things have been happening. For instance, someone has been interfering with local television broadcasting. People from this whole area are complaining of seeing a large fish on their screens and hearing a voice speaking of a fish patrol."

Bruno turned a sickly shade of grey. His mouth moved, but no sound emerged.

"Tonight," Mr. Sturgeon went on, "the voice talked about some things that appear to have something to do with Macdonald Hall." His voice took on a firm tone. "I have no proof, of course, so I am not making any accusations. My message is this: Tomorrow morning, classes will be delayed. At nine o'clock sharp, there will be a complete and thorough inspection of every room, made by me personally. I had better find everything in perfect order."

"Yes, sir," Bruno barely whispered.

"That will be all," said Mr. Sturgeon, standing up. "You are dismissed."

Bruno left the headmaster's house and dashed across the campus. By the time he reached Room 201, he was breathless and even paler than before.

"Bruno, what's wrong? What happened?" cried Boots.

"It's a good thing Elmer's away on that overnight field trip," panted Bruno. "If he were here, I'd mangle him!" He rushed over to the video machine and began pulling out wires. "Every time I've used this piece of garbage, I've been on television!"

Boots collapsed onto his bed. "Oh, no!"

"Oh, yes!" cried Bruno. "This thing was broadcasting to the whole area! Wait till I get my hands on Elmer!"

"The Fish knows!" moaned Boots.

"The Fish suspects," corrected Bruno. He began to calm down. "Tomorrow morning, there's going to be a big dorm inspection. By that time, this video machine and all the other junk in this room are going to be gone!"

"Everything?" asked Boots.

"Everything," said Bruno grimly, "except the ants and plants and fish. Even when he's angry, Mr. Sturgeon wouldn't want us killing things."

"But what about Elmer?" asked Boots. "These things are his. He'll have a fit when he gets back."

"Either he gets upset or we all get expelled," said Bruno. "Take your choice."

"But what are we going to do with everything?" demanded Boots, beginning to panic.

"We can bury it in the big sand pit by the road," decided Bruno. "The one we use for high jumping."

"There's so much of it!" moaned Boots. "It'll take us a month to bury all this!"

"That's why we have to have help," said Bruno. "We'll ask some of the guys. Right now."

The two boys got up and headed for the door.

"I don't believe it!" muttered Bruno, looking back at the video machine. "I just don't believe it!"

* * *

Shortly after midnight, Bruno and Boots and six other boys began to carry all of Elmer's experiments and equipment out of Dormitory 2. They headed for the large sand pit by the road. When they got there, they found several tired-looking boys standing beside a big hole.

"Dump everything in," ordered Bruno. "Boots, did you bring the salmon poster?"

"Yeah," Boots replied. "The stack of them he had in his dresser too."

"Good," said Bruno. "If The Fish ever sees them . . ."

The video machine went into the hole first. Wires and cables followed. Then the entire contents of Elmer's chemistry lab, including what was left of his cure for the common cold. Bottles broke and chemicals spilled out, mixing together in the sand. On top of that, they dumped the remains of Operation Flying Fish

— the remote-control box and the launcher. Then they shoved in all sorts of beakers and test tubes, some full, some empty. Elmer's salmon posters topped the smelly mess.

"That's all of it," panted Boots.

"Good," sighed Bruno. "Let's cover it up."

The boys heaped sand on top of Elmer's life's work. Then they headed quickly and quietly back to their rooms.

"Poor Elmer," muttered Boots.

"At least he won't get expelled," Bruno pointed out. "And neither will we."

Chapter 12

Take cover!

By the side of the road leading to Macdonald Hall, a soft bubbling noise rose from the sand pit where the boys had buried Elmer's experiments. Silently, without headlights, seven cars pulled onto the gravel shoulder nearby. Several figures emerged, but no one noticed the whisps of smoke rising from the mound.

The Royal Canadian Mounted Police had finally traced the strange fish broadcasts to Macdonald Hall. Now they were there with one purpose — to get their man.

"Okay," said Sergeant Harold P. Featherstone Jr., "this is it. I want the whole campus surrounded. No one goes in or out."

The men moved off to take up their assigned positions. Featherstone and two other officers climbed back into one of the cars. They drove towards the only building with a light showing, stopped the car in front of it and got out.

Mr. Sturgeon came out to greet them. "Good evening," he said. "You must be from the developer's office. I was told to expect you."

"Are you in charge here?" asked Featherstone.

"Yes, I'm the headmaster. Sturgeon is my name."

"Sturgeon!" exclaimed Featherstone. "That's a kind of fish, isn't it?"

"How clever of you," Mr. Sturgeon remarked. He eyed Featherstone coldly.

Whipping out his badge, Featherstone announced, "We've got you now, Fish!"

Mr. Sturgeon stared at him. "I beg your pardon?"

"Do you think we don't know what you've been doing? Did you think you could get away with it forever?" Featherstone was enjoying this. "We've got you now! You and your Fish Patrol are finished! Cuff him," he said to the taller of the two officers.

The office stepped forward and swiftly handcuffed himself to Mr. Sturgeon.

The headmaster was furious. "What in the world do you think —"

Featherstone reached into the car and produced a megaphone. "*Attention!*" his voice boomed across the campus. "*Macdonald Hall is now under restriction! No one is to enter or leave the grounds! Repeat, no one is allowed to enter or leave!*"

"If you would kindly explain," Mr. Sturgeon insisted.

"You'll get all the explanations you want," snapped Featherstone, "in front of a judge!"

"But —"

The announcement had aroused the boys of Macdonald Hall. A swarm of them, led by Bruno, ran onto the scene.

"Look!" shouted Bruno. "Those guys have busted The Fish!"

Featherstone turned to one of the other officers. "Did you hear that? Even the kids know he's the Fish. There's nothing worse than involving kids in crime."

"This is all a mistake!" insisted Mr. Sturgeon.

"Yeah, and you made it," said Featherstone.

By now, the entire population of Macdonald

Hall had gathered on the lawn. "Let him go!" bellowed Bruno. "Whatever it is, he didn't do it!"

Mr. Sturgeon was still trying to reason with Featherstone. "Officer, if you will just listen to me!"

"You'll have plenty of time to talk," shouted Featherstone over the noise, "when we get you and your Fish Patrol down to the station."

Across the road, Miss Scrimmage's PA system burst into life. Cathy Burton's voice crackled loudly: *"Attention, girls! Macdonald Hall is being invaded! They need our help! Let's go!"*

Instantly, a stream of girls burst out through the door and thundered across the highway to Macdonald Hall. On her balcony, Miss Scrimmage stood screaming at them. "Girls! Girls, come back here at once! Please come back!"

A strange and unexpected silence followed as everyone looked up at Miss Scrimmage. For a moment, a loud hiss could be heard from the sand pit by the road. It faded quickly and silence fell again. Then, suddenly, Elmer screamed, *"Oh, no! Take cover."*

At that very moment, there was a huge explosion. The entire sand pit rose upward in a giant fireball, lighting up the dark campus. Sand shot into the air, mixed with bits of the buried equipment.

A second explosion followed, then a third, and finally one that looked like a brilliant fireworks display. When it was over, the crowd was covered in pieces of charred salmon posters.

From her balcony, Miss Scrimmage gazed down in horror. "Help! Police!" she wailed.

"Everybody remain calm!" shouted Featherstone over the megaphone. *"This is —"* Then the wind caught a salmon poster and slapped it up against his face.

"Look!" exclaimed Boots breathlessly, pointing to the road. The highway was choked with cars. The CHUT-TV mobile unit pulled up, followed by other members of the media. Everyone was hoping to get in on a fast-breaking story.

Cathy Burton called to the crowd of reporters. "Right over there!" She pointed to the flagpole, where Mr. Sturgeon and the three

police officers stood in the centre of a crowd of confused students. "That's where the story is! By the flagpole! Over there!"

Several cameras focused on Mr. Sturgeon. Reporters stood there, waiting for him to speak. Bruno Walton pushed his way through the crowd and ran up to him. "I confess," he cried. "It's all my fault!"

Boots burst onto the scene and ran to Bruno's side. "And mine!"

Elmer Drimsdale appeared. "No!" he shouted. "I am responsible!"

Mr. Sturgeon gathered himself at last. "Remove these ridiculous handcuffs at once," he ordered.

Hopelessly confused, Sergeant Featherstone nodded feebly. The cuffs came off.

"You see," Bruno was explaining to the crowd of media, "it all started when we found out that Macdonald Hall was going broke."

"Walton, that will do," said Mr. Sturgeon.

Bruno turned towards the headmaster. "I don't think so, sir," he said. "Even though it's too late, I think everybody should know about

Macdonald Hall. They should know how a good school can go under and nobody knows or cares."

"*We care!*" chorused the students from Macdonald Hall and Miss Scrimmage's.

"We sure do!" exclaimed Bruno. "And all of us have been trying to help. We were trying to become famous, so more students would enrol here and the school would be saved. But everything we did turned out wrong. We couldn't set a world record, or be the home of some great invention. We couldn't get the publicity we needed to save the school. It just didn't work out."

"What a human interest story!" exclaimed one of the reporters. "Go on! Go on!"

"Elmer was trying to invent a new kind of video," Bruno continued, "and I was playing with it. I didn't know it was showing that fish on every TV in the whole county! We had to bury it so we wouldn't get into trouble. We buried it and the rest of Elmer's stuff in the sand pit that used to be over there. I guess the chemicals got mixed up with the wires or something, and it blew up."

"So where do the police come in?" asked one of the reporters.

Featherstone snapped out of his trance. "Ah — yes," he began. "We were — uh — looking into — uh —"

"Oh, I get it," said the reporter. "You were helping the school get publicity."

"Uh — right," he agreed.

"Hey," said a photographer, "seeing as we missed the fireworks, let's get a shot of one of you police guys shaking hands with the headmaster."

Another photographer walked up to Bruno. "I'd like a shot of you and your two friends with the headmaster."

Cameras clicked, pencils scribbled, videotapes rolled. It was two hours before Mr. Sturgeon finally called a halt to the press conference. Then he cleared the campus and sent his boys to bed.

Chapter 13

Macdonald Hall is saved

"We're doomed!" muttered Boots as he, Bruno and Elmer walked towards the headmaster's office. Classes had been cancelled for the day because of the state of the grounds, but Mr. Sturgeon had sent for the three boys right after lunch.

"I don't care," said Bruno. "Macdonald Hall is gone, but at least we sent it out with a bang." He reached down and picked up a slightly burned salmon poster. "Here, Elmer."

"Thank you," said Elmer weakly. "Do you think we'll be expelled?"

"You can't be expelled from a school that doesn't exist," moaned Bruno. "We'll just go before everybody else, that's all."

They entered the building and marched to the office. Mr. Sturgeon met them and invited them inside. He seated them on the visitors' chairs rather than on the hard bench.

Mr. Sturgeon pointed to a stack of newspapers on his desk. "You boys made quite an impression last night." He began to read the headlines: *"Loyal Students Fight to Save School . . . Save Our School, Cry Macdonald Hall Boys . . . Fight to Save School Ends in Explosion . . .* The list is endless. You were on local and network TV last night. Two major magazines want to do articles on Macdonald Hall, and the *Science Gazette* would like to talk to you, Drimsdale."

The three boys stared in silence.

"I have some good news for all of us," Mr. Sturgeon went on. "This morning alone we have had hundreds of telephone calls from parents all over the country. Already over forty new boys have been signed up for next year. We expect many more."

"Hooray!" blurted Bruno, jumping to his feet. He sat down quickly. "I mean — uh — that's very nice."

Mr. Sturgeon beamed. "Very nice indeed," he agreed. "We are planning to reopen Dormitory 3. We may even build a Dormitory 4. So I would like to thank you for your efforts."

"I'm not going to be expelled then, sir?" asked Elmer hopefully.

"Hardly," said Mr. Sturgeon. "I would even guess that you may become famous. The *Science Gazette* is very interested in your video system. They wonder how you could overpower the CHUT-TV transmitter."

Elmer blushed. "It wasn't supposed to do that."

"While we're on the subject, boys," said the headmaster, "there are a few things I would like to have explained." He cleared his throat carefully. "Recently, I have received a series of complaints from Miss Scrimmage. For instance, does anyone know if she was actually, as she phrased it, 'attacked'?"

"That would have to be when Boots fell on her," offered Bruno.

"It was an accident, sir," added Boots quickly.

Mr. Sturgeon nodded slowly. "What about her story that a member of the Macdonald Hall staff was running around her school in his underclothes?"

"Oh, that was just Coach Flynn, sir," said Bruno. "But it was his gym shorts, not his underwear. He doesn't know anything about it, though. He was asleep at the time."

"I beg your pardon?" snapped Mr. Sturgeon.

"You see," explained Boots, "we put Elmer's cold cure in his Muscle-Ade and he drank it. He started to hiccup and fell asleep. Then he went sleepwalking. But it wasn't his fault."

"Is there anything else you'd like to know about, sir?" asked Bruno.

"Just one more thing comes to mind," said the headmaster. "Would there be anything in Elmer Drimsdale's equipment that might have caused Miss Scrimmage to see a red and green flying bomb?"

Elmer choked and had to be pounded on the back by his two roommates.

"It was the *M.H.Flying* — uh — a remote-control device, sir," said Bruno.

"Ah, yes," said Mr. Sturgeon. "That would be the flying fish, the one that flew away."

"Yes, sir."

"I see. That will be all, then," said Mr.

Sturgeon. "You are dismissed. Next time, I suggest that you inform me and get permission for your activities. Good day."

* * *

Saturday dawned warm and sunny. The boys had slept in after their big victory party.

Boots eased himself out of bed and walked over to the window. He looked out, then stared. "Bruno — Bruno, I think you'd better see this."

"See what?" asked Bruno.

"Come and see," Boots insisted.

Bruno stumbled over to the window and looked out. He let out a bellow of rage. There, on Miss Scrimmage's front lawn, shone the world's largest pop-can pyramid. It was more than five metres tall. Parked in front of the gates was the CHUT-TV mobile unit. Right behind it was a large, blue van. The words *Rankin Book of World Records* were painted on the side.

"My pyramid!" shrieked Bruno. "They stole my pyramid!" Before Boots could stop him, he had scrambled out the window and was running across the campus in his pyjamas.